Peabody Public Library
Columbia City, IN

A Rookie reader®

W9-AVI-654

My **Special** Space

Written by Dana Meachen Rau

Illustrated by Julie J. Kim

DISCARD

JE PAPER RAU
Rau, Dana Meachen,
My special space / written
by Dana Meachen Rau ;
illustrated by Julie J. Kim.

NOV 30 '09

Children's Press®
A Division of Scholastic Inc.
New York • Toronto • London • Auckland • Sydney
Mexico City • New Delhi • Hong Kong
Danbury, Connecticut

4

For Chris, Charlie, and Allison,
who let me have a special space,
and often get invited in
—D.M.R.

For my greatest blessing...my family
—J.J.K.

Reading Consultants

Linda Cornwell
Literacy Specialist

Katharine A. Kane
Education Consultant
(Retired, San Diego County Office of Education
and San Diego State University)

Library of Congress Cataloging-in-Publication Data

Rau, Dana Meachen, 1971-
  My special space / written by Dana Meachen Rau ;
illustrated by Julie J. Kim.- 1st American ed.
      p. cm. — (Rookie reader)
Summary: A girl describes the hideaway in her closet where she goes when
she wants to spend time by herself.
  ISBN 0-516-22881-1 (lib. bdg.)   0-516-27788-X (pbk.)
  [1. Solitude—Fiction. 2. Clothes closets—Fiction. 3. Stories in rhyme.]
I. Kim, Julie J., 1973- ill. II. Title. III. Series.
  PZ8.3.R232My 2003
  [E]—dc21
                        2003003887

© 2003 by Dana Meachen Rau
Illustrations © 2003 by Julie J. Kim
All rights reserved. Published simultaneously in Canada.
Printed in the United States of America.

CHILDREN'S PRESS, and A ROOKIE READER®, and associated logos are trademarks and or
registered trademarks of Scholastic Library Publishing. SCHOLASTIC and associated logos
are trademarks and or registered trademarks of Scholastic Inc.
1 2 3 4 5 6 7 8 9 10 R 12 11 10 09 08 07 06 05 04 03

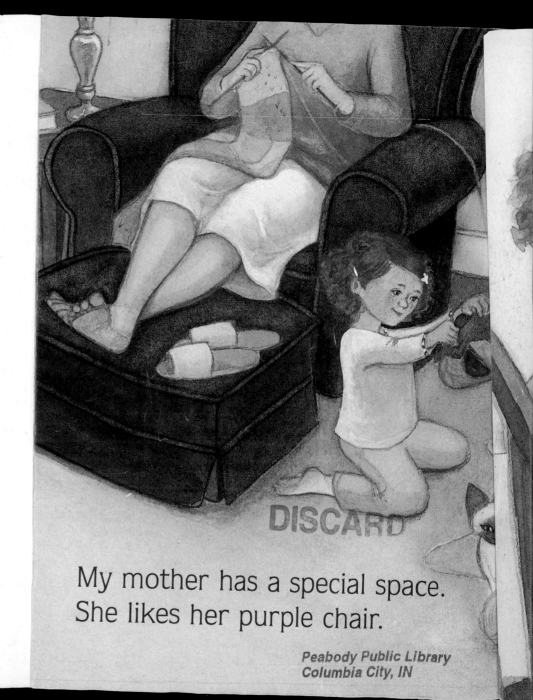

My mother has a special space.
She likes her purple chair.

Peabody Public Library
Columbia City, IN

My father likes the table.
He reads the paper there.

6

My brother likes the tree house.

My sister likes the floor.

9

My pets have special spaces
behind the kitchen door.

My special space is somewhere
I can be all by myself.

I have pillows there,
my blanket, too,
and drawings on the shelf.

14

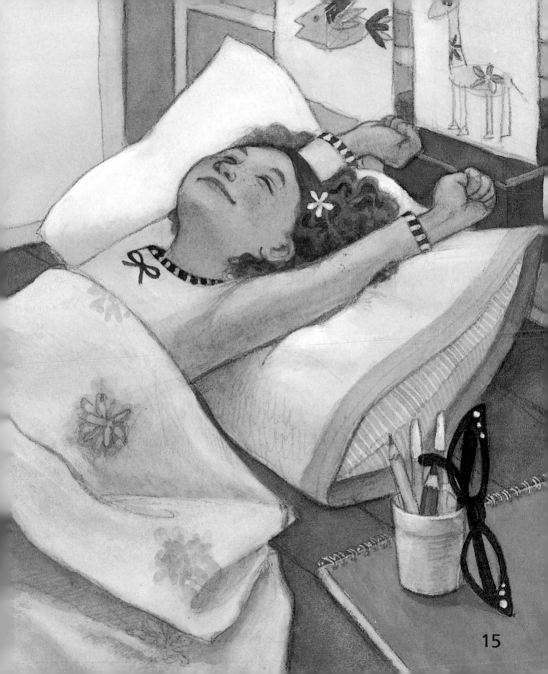

Sometimes I like to daydream.

Sometimes I read my books.

Sometimes I do my homework
or practice funny looks.

Sometimes I play with puzzles.

23

Sometimes I sing off-key.

It's okay to make mistakes
because it's only me.

But sometimes it's too quiet
in my secret hiding place.

That's when I invite a friend
to share my special space.

Peabody Public Library
Columbia City, IN

Word List (80 words)

a	drawings	it's	or	sing
all	father	key	paper	sister
and	floor	kitchen	pets	sometimes
be	friend	like	pillows	somewhere
because	funny	likes	place	space
behind	has	looks	play	spaces
blanket	have	make	practice	special
books	he	me	purple	table
brother	her	mistakes	puzzles	that's
but	hiding	mother	quiet	the
by	homework	my	read	there
can	house	myself	reads	to
chair	I	off	secret	too
daydream	in	okay	share	tree
do	invite	on	she	when
door	is	only	shelf	with

About the Author

When Dana Meachen Rau was a child, she would hide in a special space in her closet. Today, her favorite special space is the sunny spot at the foot of her bed. Dana has written more than seventy-five books for children, including early readers, biographies, nonfiction, and storybooks. She lives in Burlington, Connecticut, with her husband Chris, and children Charlie and Allison.

About the Illustrator

Julie Kim lives and paints in Seattle, Washington, rain or shine.

DISCARD

Peabody Public Library
Columbia City, IN